"In this life, it often seems like we are all just crazy pitchers swinging for the fences with our wild fastballs of hectic imagination, and Victor Clevenger is no exception, a child of that chaos, with all of its troubled patriotism turned inward, taken apart and put back together here piece by piece, *Disordered Portion* is simply that, one man's heart, with all of its interchangeable parts, a jigsaw puzzle of lyrical emotion, that reminds us all—exactly what it means to be free."

— **John Dorsey**, author of *Your Daughter's Country*

"Not the midwest nice of the folksy plains, nor the romanticized grit of the mythologized middle America, Victor Clevenger's poetry is the voice of the real working-class American man. Not a plastic-patriotic Chevy Truck commercial. Not an over-produced, posturing country music millionaire, Clevenger's authenticity, his manhood, is in his vulnerability. His writing is tender, but not sentimental, empathetic, but not patronizing. You can feel his knuckles turn white as he grapples with his past, transcending through the pen. He is a father who confesses his demons to his children, not with some faux-patriarchal posing, but as a man who dug his own grave and pulled himself out."

— **Chase Dimock**, author of *Sentinel Species*, editor of *As It Ought To Be Magazine*

"A lot of people don't understand, but Victor Clevenger is not a poet, not really, he's a photographer with no camera. And this is not a collection of poems, it is an album full of high end photos of low-brow culture and hard living, Instagrams and Polaroids of the good times and bad times, the desperate dreams and grinning acts of defiance and genuine moments of beauty, all seen through the eyes of the 21st century American everyman who's just trying to get by and make sense of it all."

— **Jason Ryberg**, editor of *Spartan Press*

"This new collection is perfect for the times we find ourselves in, poems with unflinching honesty in their every inspired word. I've always been a fan of Victor's work and consider this new book his very best because he confronts personal issues in poems that shine a light on the impressive, beautiful courage of his righteous humanity. I am really inspired by these poems and consider them the work of a master poet who is authentic, soulful and a worthy hero at a time when the world needs the same kind of gritty realism and hard-fought wisdom found in poems that have a stubborn hope that glows in the dark."

— **Kevin Ridgeway**, author of *Too Young to Know*

DISORDERED PORTION

New and Selected Poems
by Victor Clevenger

ISBN: 978-93-88319-45-4

First Edition: 2020

Rs. 200/-

Cyberwit.net

HIG 45 Kaushambi Kunj, Kalindipuram

Allahabad - 211011 (U.P.) India

http://www.cyberwit.net

Tel: +(91) 9415091004

E-mail: info@cyberwit.net

Printed at Thomson Press India Limited.

Disordered Portion contains three new poems from the unpublished collection, *47 Poems*, & three selected poems from each the following books: *In All These Naked Pictures Of Us* (IP, 2016), *Come Here* (Least Bittern Books, 2016), *The More Exciting Side Of Death* (Epic Rites Press, 2016), *SOULWHORE* (Svensk Apache Press, 2017), *Congenital Pipe Dreams* (Spartan Press, 2017), *Sandpaper Lovin'* (Crisis Chronicles Press, 2017), *Resurrection of a Sunflower*, (Pski's Porch, 2017), *Tom Farris is My Brother* (CWP Collective Press, 2017), *Her Bastard Soul* (Epic Rites Press, 2017), *Ginger Roots Are Best Taken Orally*, with Tom Farris (EMP, 2018), *A Finger in the Hornets' Nest* (Red Flag Press, 2018), *On The Tip Of Our Tongues* (Analog Submission Press, 2018), *Corned Beef Hash by Candlelight* (Luchador Press, 2019), *Dog Park 2* (River Dog, 2020), *Low-Flying Birds* (River Dog, 2020), *A Walk Down Mammary Lane* (Analog Submission Press, 2020), *The Ghosts of Our Words Will be Heroes in Hell*, with John Dorsey, Jason Ryberg, & Damian Rucci (OAC Books, 2020) & *A Wildflower in Blood* (Roaring Junior Press, 2020).

Grateful acknowledgment is given to all these fine publishers & presses, including Rat's Ass Review, Yellow Chair Review, The Gasconade Review, As It Ought To Be Magazine, & Bad Acid Inc., where some of these poems first appeared in various forms.

Contents:

I'm a Writer, not a Fighter

& on the nights when
my busted lips
   tint the ice cubes red

  & she sits there for an hour
letting the melted water
      run down
her soft cold fingers

 i tell her
   even superheroes take a few
  good punches   darling
nobody can dodge them all

she always laughs kindly
then reminds me
  sweetheart   i have yet to see
        you dodge one

Beating Winter Moments with Summer Memories

i remember
standing
in a
crowded
market
& the
people
surrounding
me
were
ugly

the
children
were
ugly

they were
standing
in lines
with their
parents

the men
were
ugly

the women
were

ugly

i was
standing
in line
with my
parents
& we
were
ugly too

it was
a cold
morning
&
everyone
was
dressed
for the weather:
long pants
long sleeves
hats
scarves
gloves

it was a
hopeless
gathering
of disgust

i took
my gloves
off to pluck

a petal loose
from the
fresh roses
that were
wrapped
in plastic
at the end
of aisle 3

that petal
was
nothing
like
the crowd

i rubbed it
between my
fingers
& it was soft

it
reminded
me of
beautiful
things

like warm
cotton candy
or the
babysitter's
legs
under the

covers
when
i
was
seven

Eating Religion

stomach
hearts
heads
& souls

all
swollen
&
bloated up
like
wet rice

it all
produces
shit

day after day

Come Here Poem

in a great flash of hunger
darling   the stars in the sky
will one day devour us all
with passion & purpose

Come Here Poem

before alcoholism   my
toughest
addiction was
my love for the
manic inside of
a depressive
woman

Come Here Poem

you beat upon my
heart with both
fists

you are my favorite bruise

Most Nights

the most
important
thing

is
her
cocktail glass

When I was an Older Boy

smack-dab in the pubescent
choke hold & accompanying
powerbomb

growing thin ginger hued hair
on my lip & on my chin
awkward   walking around
with a body covered in acne
like an active minefield

half detonated with scabbed &
scarred casualties left lying in
the sun   salicylic acid 2%
covering them

horny & inexperienced—
i dreamt of a woman sitting
naked   straddling my face like
they do in fuck-films

lora   my first   slightly shorter
in height than i was   smack-dab
in the choke hold & powerbomb
herself   had dark hair

smelt like a cherry field &
showed me on the day that i lost my
virginity that dreams can come true
when she straddled up on me

i let my tongue loose with a fury
of punches like a prizefighter
            swinging blindly

& When

you have
finally
figured it out

you will wake
up sober
& remember
nothing

it's okay

life is laughing
at us all

I Kissed

your forehead
& naked stomach
before i climbed out
of bed this
morning

& i could still smell
the md 20/20 in the
air from your
breath

you swallowed enough
last night

that you started
to recite poetry

& i have come to the
conclusion:

you just might be
my soulwhore

Just Crawling

bare chested
through
wet grass

in night's darkness

hoping the
worm's path
brings sense

before the
morning sun
leaves you dry

& stepped
over

by this city

Sometimes

a fat lip is the prize that tomorrow will bring

Why I Preferred Bastard Friends

i was the type of little squirt who exclusively
enjoyed my own pillow with baseballs on
the case   blankets with tigers creeping
through trees   that worn down mattress that
sunk deep in the middle   & the four walls
that surrounded it all

so i was out-of-my comfort zone when i
spent the night   for the first time   with him
but the evening eased along decently as we
ate cheese pizza   watched hulk hogan body
slam andre at mania 3   built a fort with
bedsheets tied to the knobs of his dresser
drawers   & fell asleep before his older
brother came home at curfew & stumbled
across the bedroom floor

in the morning we woke up early   lifted his
bedroom window which was on the second
floor   spotted a small brown bird   & wasted
it with his slingshot & a red marble   feathers
flew everywhere as we ran quickly down the
stairs to tell the story to anyone   but his
angry father stopped us halfway through the
story & began smacking his hands against
the back of our heads for being what he
called *stupid lil' sonz-uh-bitches* & we
cowered upstairs in the fort until my mother
got there at noon

I'm Writing

all of our
love scenes
in the
beginning

because
gunshots
make better
movie plots

& i fully
expect
the closing
credits

to scroll
across a
photograph

of a
tombstone
that reads:

some holes
are opened
with intentions
of never being
closed

Darkness & Solitude

kick me in the teeth
until my choppers
crumble into dust

& i spit them out
like spilled sugar
onto the nightstand

just to say   *hello*

to the morning sun-
shine peering through
my windows with

bittersweet
greetings & groans

Feeding My Demons

i hated looking at my ugliness each morning
in the mirror   i was convinced that there were
small demons living inside of me   so i would
drink every day   & then every night i was drunk

i would hold her body down against the bed's
blankets   against the living room's carpet
against the car's front seats   against the hallway's
stairs   or against the lamp post that stood outside

i would squeeze her wrists with a persuasive force
heavy enough to crush plums in my palms & it would
leave filthy-finger marks on her skin

she was never defiant during these times   & i
would beg for her love with hot sangria breath

she would tell me with her gentle voice   be kind
don't be an asshole   this world already has plenty of
assholes

i would let loose of her soon after this
& then we would finally cook dinner

we never ate before midnight

Love Letters

i blamed her   because someone had to be blamed &
it didn't matter what she tried to say—i goddamn
swore to her face that she had found them   & did as
any jealous lover would have done   destroyed them
& denied ever knowing their existence

she denied knowing their existence   of course   &
when i told her that they were last hidden in the
bottom of a cooking pot   which was in the bottom of
the large box that had some other old pots & frying
pans on the top of it   she laughed

why are you laughing   because just the other day i
gave that large box to the lady next door who was
collecting things for the church   she replied

what church   the baptist church around the corner
she said   i hurried to put on my jacket & told her i
spent years wrapping them in bundles & hiding them
in different places   so that each new woman
couldn't find them   & you ruined it   you ruined
them

i rushed out the door before she could say another
word   & once i made it to the church steps   every
door was locked   i walked around the drive twice
before i found the trashcans hidden behind a picket
fence

i climbed the fence   & in the bottom of the third can

that i tipped over were my old love letters that i had
never sent   but saved   i sat down on the gravel &
opened one

it was one that i had written last year to michelle   it
was written in all capital letters & the beginning said:

OF COURSE I'M NOT PERFECT   CHRIST   IS
THAT WHAT YOU THOUGHT   THAT I WAS
PERFECT

i sat there wishing that i had given that letter to her
i wished that i had given all the letters to all the
women i had written them for   & vowed that one
day   i still may   but on that day   i just walked
back home

& waited for her to leave   so that i could hide the
letters once again   & if she is to find them   then so
be it   i guess she will know my misery

November 10th

i was hungry   but couldn't eat   i swallowed two
more vicodin (pretending that the first pill was
potatoes & that the second pill was hot brown gravy)
they both hit an empty pit in my stomach   as my
tongue rubbed against each tooth that remained
another dry socket   & i sat confused with three
socks—two white socks on my feet & a black sock on
my left hand   i'm right hand dominate   i have
always been right hand dominate.

the weather man inside the clock radio said
prepare for a night colder than any night we have
seen yet this year   & can someone please check on
the homeless   there was a shelter that closed its
doors today

pocket change   the chiron review issue #97   an old
pair of eyeglasses   a stained coffee cup   a stained
wine glass   animal crackers   & i scratched what was
left of this pencil with the only sharp object i could
find in all the clutter that was lying on the
nightstand—a pair of fingernail clippers became dull
with lead dust   but i had exposed enough to write
with   & enough was simply all i needed   i wrote
despite the ache in my head   i wrote slowly
i wrote

*— sometimes you just have to laugh at
responsibility & then slaughter it   be bold & do it
like i do it . . . choke it with dirty fingers*

& then bury it under some broken acorns & oak
leaves near the trees that all the stray dogs piss on
i know it all sounds crazy & makes no sense   but
sometimes it has to happen that way   you gotta
make it a goddamn horror show & satisfy yourself
the last time that i slaughtered responsibility   i sat
across the street in my car with the window down
smoking newports until i saw the stray dogs coming   &
then i was satisfied   i drove home   & washed my dirty
fingers back clean before i dialed her phone number   she
answered   & i told her   baby   i am ready to love you
again —

by this point the pencil needed worked over with the
nail clippers   but i didn't have the desire to work it
over   i had the desire to smoke a cigarette   & even
though i knew that my desire to smoke cigarettes was
fully responsible for my aching predicament   i once
again chose to slaughter responsibility for desire   &
as i sat there inhaling through the misery   the frost
danced designs all over the windows outside & the
voice inside the clock radio said

it's now twenty-nine degrees in the city   & by
request   this next song goes out to amanda   who
lives on the east side of kansas city
paul loves you

Love

is a wildflower
growing mad

all over the hillsides
of every man's soul

Absinthe O' Blue

the sky is a glum color
of battered reality

dreams   oh beautiful dreams
turn to nightmares

as the prostitute puts on her shoes
& returns to the streets
you could never pave in gold
for her

A Noose of Fingertips

close to meeting death last night
tobacco pipe pressed against lips
as he tried to strangle himself
repeatedly with his own two hands

a few times he had a pretty good grip
on himself & he squeezed hard
until he started to see streaks of colors
jumping through his eyelids

when the colors jumped he would try
to squeeze even harder but each time
he squeezed harder his ears would pop
& he would fall down to the floor

he gave up on trying & cried tears
that were thicker & harder than rock salt
when he woke the next morning
he had a headache & he asked god
to give him strength

he swears that god laughed out loud

1993

during the daytime
he would mimic his mother
giving thanks for all
things no matter
how small
he mastered his smile
in the shiny reflection of
anything he gazed upon &
during the nighttime
he would mimic his
father
shifting weight from
side to side with clenched fist
shaking them at the
demons inside of himself
from behind his closed
bedroom door
he was his teachers' favorite
student
he was his neighbors'
paper boy
he was a fourteen-year-old
boy with a bottle
of gin hidden
underneath his bed
next to his bible
there wasn't dust
covering either one of them

Quiet Storm

to talk to him   he openly admitted to every damn
deficiency which manifested behind his eyes   there
were times in the daylight that his eyes greatly ached
so he learned to shadow them with ninety-nine cent
masquerade masks in the back alleyways

he wore the masks while kissing   pressing   &
rubbing his smoky hued whiskers against the cheeks
& chins & lips of his lovers as he pursued to press the
deities daily by encouraging his lovers to drop one
penny into a pint bottle

because there were never any wishing wells in the
back alleys   but there was always his dirty-hot-hope
& he learned to deliver his dirty-hot-hope better than
any god   or goddess

eventually the pennies never left their pockets
& it didn't change a damn thing   he already had his
lovers convinced he was the greatest   & i didn't love
him   but i envied him   i was a fifteen-year-old boy
back then   i stared daily out of my bedroom window
which overlooked the alley

his lovers were mine when i closed my eyes &
moaned   at nighttime   i rubbed my face against my
pillow   softly   like a marvelous pair of tits
i worked fantasy well   i ground my hips against the
bed to the rhythm of an r&b slow jam

Deb

i used to wake her
late at night
& we would shower
together washing
each other clean
prior to sitting outside
& smoking small cigarettes
as we gazed the sky
for falling stars

i haven't seen her
in three years

our son
hasn't seen her either

She Knew

that for
her

there was
a tiny
devil

inside every
bottle

consistently
swallowing

she freed
them
all

As Always

it was
too much
midweek

with a lot

of yesterday
afternoon

You Have to Give

up at times
just to continue

pull the pillow
over your
head

suck your lungs
full

& scream hard
without making
a sound

my throat bleeds
daily

XII.

weed with Mandy
a dirt road bridge
skipping English class
kissing under a hot sun

in a wicked garden
dreaming of
responsibilities

that we would now
gladly give away

X.

for john dorsey

chicken
chicken fried chicken
food of saints
sinners enjoy too
why all this religious
bullshit in the world
when we could all
just eat breakfast in peace

XXV.

inside
like a
thief

burning
the jeweled
box

sparks ran
down my
thighs

V.

she asks me if i still have a war brain
our dirty fingers picking up garbage that two
stray cats had scattered   a black one
with a white face & an orange one
with a short tail
she looks so damn mean with a red face
& gritted teeth   she asks
do you think that you can kill them
i remember listening to the radio transmissions
working the overnight shift with sybil   i remember
holding onto her when the car bomb exploded
next to the landing zone that morning in 2005
now twenty minutes late for work already   i held
an empty tuna can like it was a lover's hand

Brandy

i wish that wishbones
were actually
more wishes
than bones

I Fear

that one
day

we may all
begin to
bleed
out

while the
paramedics
diagnose
us

as the
generations

who should
have known
better

Forced Sober

days are getting rougher
miles growing greater
distance is the demon's chin i swing at

knockout punches in dreams
each time forget how it feels to fight
palm fist feet elbow knuckles blood
brow skin eyes lips bruised

i'm always tougher in dreams
excess muscles mind skill luck
lately they've all failed me
finished in first rounds

when i wake early i feel beaten
sore back arms legs wrists hips
standing naked in a kitchen
waiting on coffee to brew
black donut shop 12 ounce cup

sip swallow sip again
recall fragments of dream fights
i never fully remember them all
it's probably for the best

looking out the window
i tell the fading moon it's irritating
you're a whisky bottle
& it has now been two months
since i last put my hands on your curves

Reggie's Advice During My 1ˢᵗ Marriage

they're stupid
but even flies eventually give up on dead things

& move on

Nuclear Goodbyes

it's all in your tone
but that's not how you argue anymore
my children tell me
emotions in the waves of voices
have been lost in the leaps
& the bounds of convenience
it's all uppercase letters on a screen now
followed by exclamation points
to make the point
attach an emoji that is crying one tear
angry face
shades of all your frustration
attach another one crying two tears
followed by blue hearts
then red ones
that are broken in two pieces
i shake my head
because what they say is truth
i too have spoken from the gut
without saying a word
i ask my children
how their children's children
will argue with the ones they love
when those rough days
in their futures start to arrive
& they have no clue
i have no clue
guess time will tell
if they will even be given
the opportunity to quarrel

because today
there are still men building bombs
to drop from the sky
on human beings

& that is sadder
than anything i've just said

Silent in Love

we see
birds of prey circling
the spaces above
our heads

today

my heart is like a
starving lion

waiting for you to say anything
with nourishment

Beautiful Things Attract Beautiful Things
for belle

a shimmer lingers

it shows me
you're not a stranger
to the dust of burning stars

if you were to tell me
you could catch a hot one
in the palm of your hands

& hold it
like a passionate heartbeat
keeping it warm until the sun rises

i'd believe you

Meth Rock in His Pocket

my heart like a bone
laid in a woven basket like bread
ribs aged almost forty years
i know my fate
the feeling of being ripped open
by an animal's tooth doesn't saddened me anymore

bentley though
his heart's like a handful of water
falling upon the parched lips of all that follow
sometimes i just watch him
he looks like a red-haired jesus christ spreading love
in a city park

last night he asked me about his mother again
said he wished she'd just come back to see him
& i didn't know what to say
because i've never told him the truth
that four years ago she disappeared
while chasing a man with a meth rock in his pocket
& that i never tried to stop her

because i knew better
than to wage a war that i'd never win

with all the demons she had inside of her

i would have had more success
lying on my back & trying to piss
on the side of the sun

Poem for My Grandson #2

on a sidewalk stone hard hotel mattress
in farmington, missouri   i'm alone again
like sunshine at midnight never seen
traveling job blues   & in-betweens
sitting with silver rum & tonic water
in two paper cups reading
the courtyard poems by frank t. rios when
at 10:19pm your mother sent a message
to my telephone   a photograph
of you in dim lamplight
half stewed on milk & dreaming
a smile in your sleep like joy's plush blanket
drug across your bare feet   comfort
at the end of a day
when falling ice outside conspired
to hold our existence hostage
our flesh our bones our breath
captured by interior walls
& restrained by threads unseen
but neither we cried out
or shouted
for help   in fact
in that photograph you looked as happy
& content as my heart
at that very moment sending
a reply message back to your mother
at 10:20pm
i told her thank you
for thinking
about me too

Street Preacher

in grand junction, colorado
a drunk man stands in a parking lot
shouting through the windows at us
about making bad choices
as the waitress takes our order
we turn our head
ignore him & he leaves
after we're served
& take our first bites
in collective disgust we know
that he meant no harm
that he'd stumbled upon us in peace
to preach under the influence
to four damned idiots
who all ordered hamburgers
at a denny's

Contortionism

for Anna Tivel

if a man or woman could press their bones flat
into dust & magic   to be folded sharply
into a paper airplane   they would do it
underneath any dark chandelier

before begging the sun to rise tomorrow morning
over the alleyways in slow motion

for satisfaction

as they float out of control on a breeze

that began with every gentle exhale
between the words that you sang tonight

Nostalgia

summer
was suggestively better
back when we knew no laws of nature
& could easily kiss the neck
of a lightning bolt

Full of Magic

low-flying birds
see all the love fiends

down there in streetcars kissing

while needles

fall out of haystacks

Vaccine

we seem
doomed

smell like
worry

but still dream nightly

of magic

Thursday Evening in September

for nothing more
than to close an open window
i rushed into the first room on the left
with a bust-down-a-door
cop mentality

& his sudden search for concealment

reminded me why
it's always best to knock first
& wait for him to finish twisting the knob
before entering the room with caution

it doesn't always take a gunshot
or a slice from a sharp blade
to leave a scar

sometimes

it's just a hard object
gripped by a hand

Milkman's Mustache

i offer him a razor for the first time

he declines it
like a thirsty hound from hell
when offered holy water

turning his head from side to side
in front of a bathroom mirror

admiring something that looks quite fragile in its
infancy

like spiderwebs the color of rust
that spell out the word masculinity
in a thin font stretched

across his cracked lips

Tenderloins

reggie tells the milkman
that passion is multi-use seasoning
sprinkled on with best guesses
& that   it tastes savory
in the early morning
when you're still stoned &
chewing on the consequences
of having sex in a public place
with someone just as stoned & hungry
as you are

Poem for Madi

in a salina ihop
the first thing i notice is your
long legs

standing on your tippy toes
i bet you can see over the nighttime
into tomorrow

how beautiful
the sound of a distant moan

clouds kissing your neck every night
like a lover

Clevenger Painting

when piccard & jones had just flown
the first balloon non-stop around the world
i was working seven days a week
on a job site painting new homes for happy people
with more money than i had
my fingernails stained with minwax
puritan pine & early american
a mixture of shit
smeared on every set of oak cabinets
in platte county missouri spring 1999
nostrils full of hi-build lacquer & dust
ears buzzing huffing stoned
during my lunch breaks talking to tommy
who had spiked hair & a neck tattoo
a hired hand dating my cousin tonya
after he'd done some time in the penitentiary
& i was seven months into my first marriage
at that point working for the family business
so we would joke about how i was doing
a double bit of hard time myself shackled & chained
without the balls & keys to break free
but quite often i'd tell myself
four months past my turning nineteen
that i refuse to stroke myself into a corner
day after day with a thin bristled brush
that had dried up years ago
with someone else's dull
earth toned dreams

2 Lovers on South Aiken Avenue

kissing each other with mouths open wide
mashed together bodies leaning
against a telephone pole

near the closed day care center
on the corner

your hands up her shirt
& hers up yours

i'm certain that you have no clue i'm even there
waking up at 3a.m. on the concrete step
across the street half-hungover
& watching you

thinking about
how i don't feel like a creep

because there is not one single star
in the sky that is dead
& falling

they're all high & holding

watching you two
lust rub & dance

to any pittsburgh street sound
that resembles
a tune

Hot Things Are Just Cold Things with Heat

you say love
a strange   strange thing

i say it's like a frank standford poem

beautiful & wanting more

like small doves in stew pots
without vegetables

when starving
i give you my portion

& watch you smile

picking through tiny bones
like diamonds scattered

on a paper plate

After the Duck's Head Falls

after the duck's head falls
to the swing of a hatchet
& blood washes down
into the dirt's cracks
like thirsty mouths begging

i think about those quacks
that i'd heard for many months
before & wonder
how far their sound
actually traveled through hot air

did they reach that moment
where ghosts & last embers
of yesterday's stars
heard them fade crackle pop
into non-existence

or are they still there floating endlessly

silent in protest

brushing up against my cheeks
like a kiss

The Last Supper

the sun turns its back on us daily
turns a blind eye to it all

vultures fall to the ground to feast
without remorse

knowing that

while resting against filthy rib bones
a heart does not grow
like a wildflower
in blood

America, We Can't Fuck Like This Forever

without moving

our middle-aged days hold their breath
& just lay there

spread open staring

out a window

at yesterday morning

As Much as Anything Else

america
your mother wants you
to be kind

Disordered Portion

there was no money
there was only a slice of an old romance

& a side dish of chicken

a mere shadow
of reality